COLORING BOOK FOR ADULTS
(And Big Kids)

Relaxation & Stress Relieving Designs

Over 40 Symmetrical Mandalas & Geometric Patterns

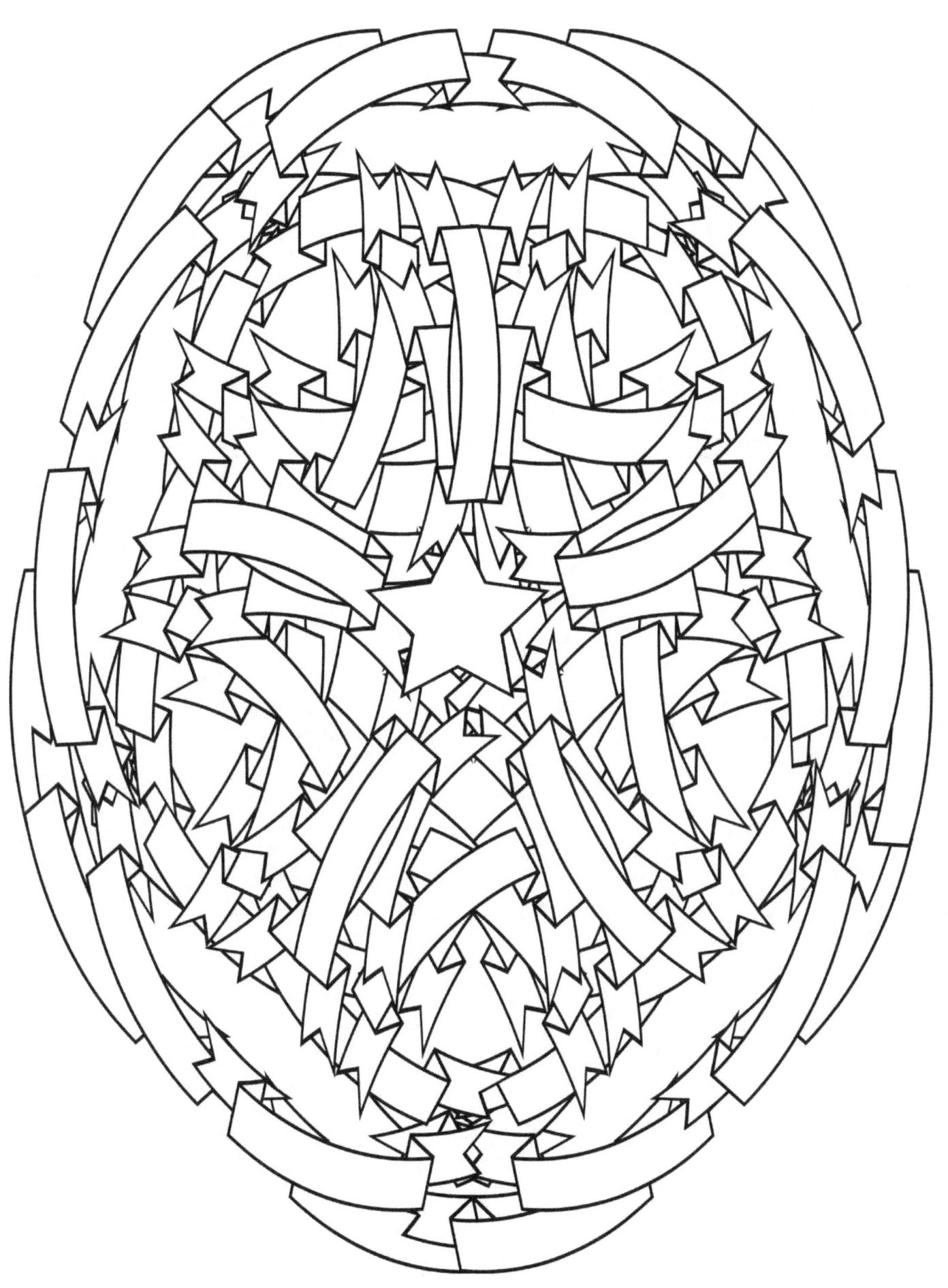

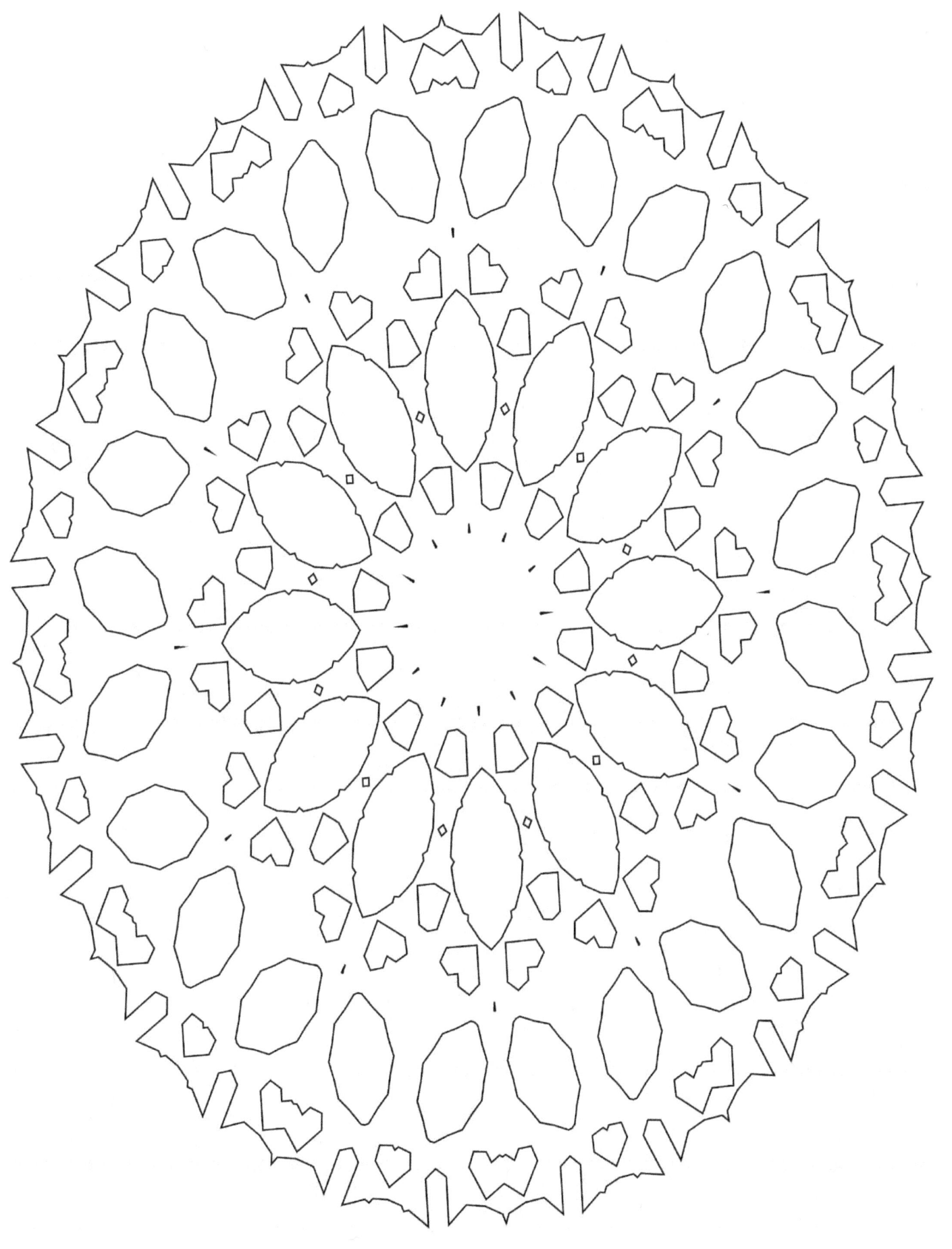

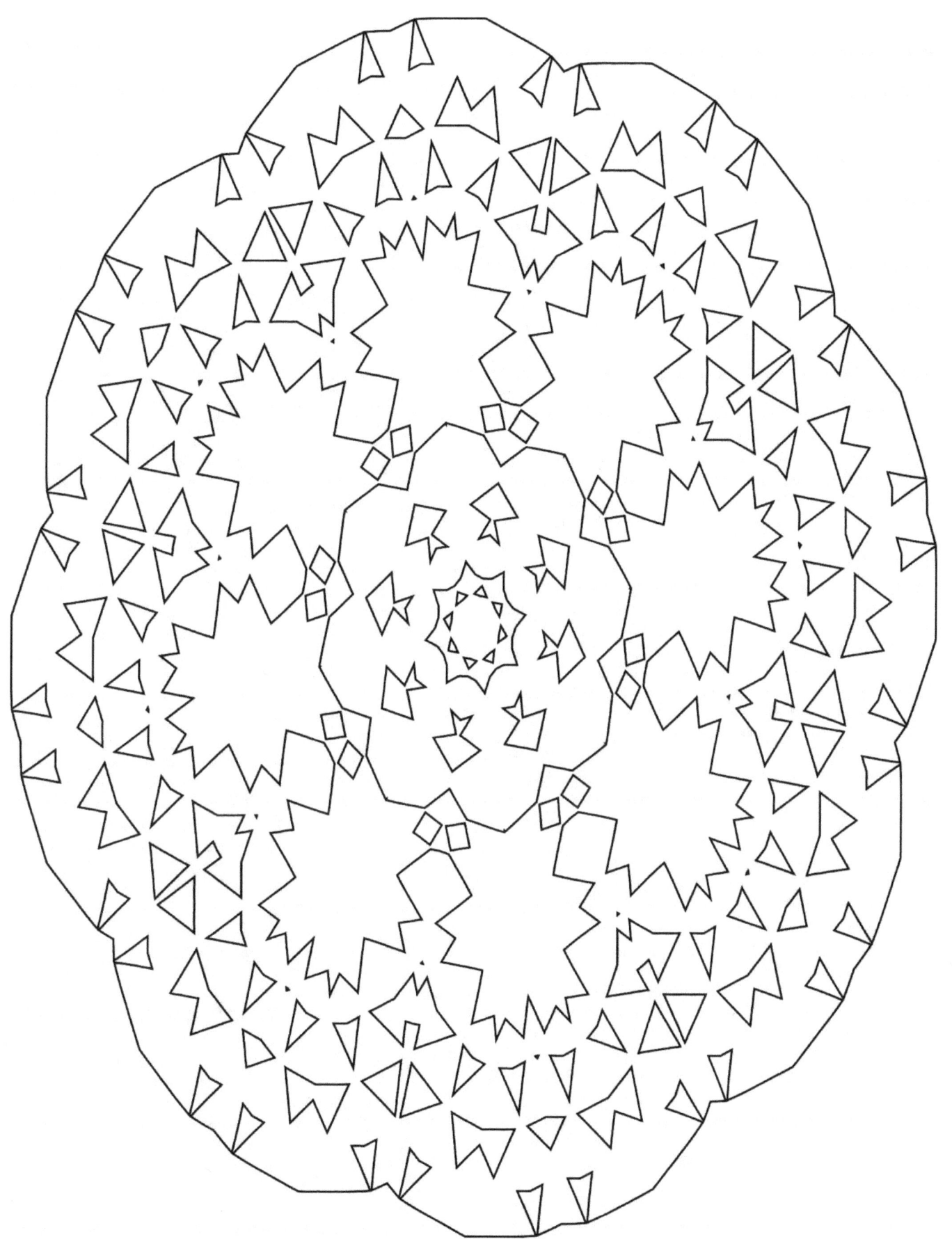

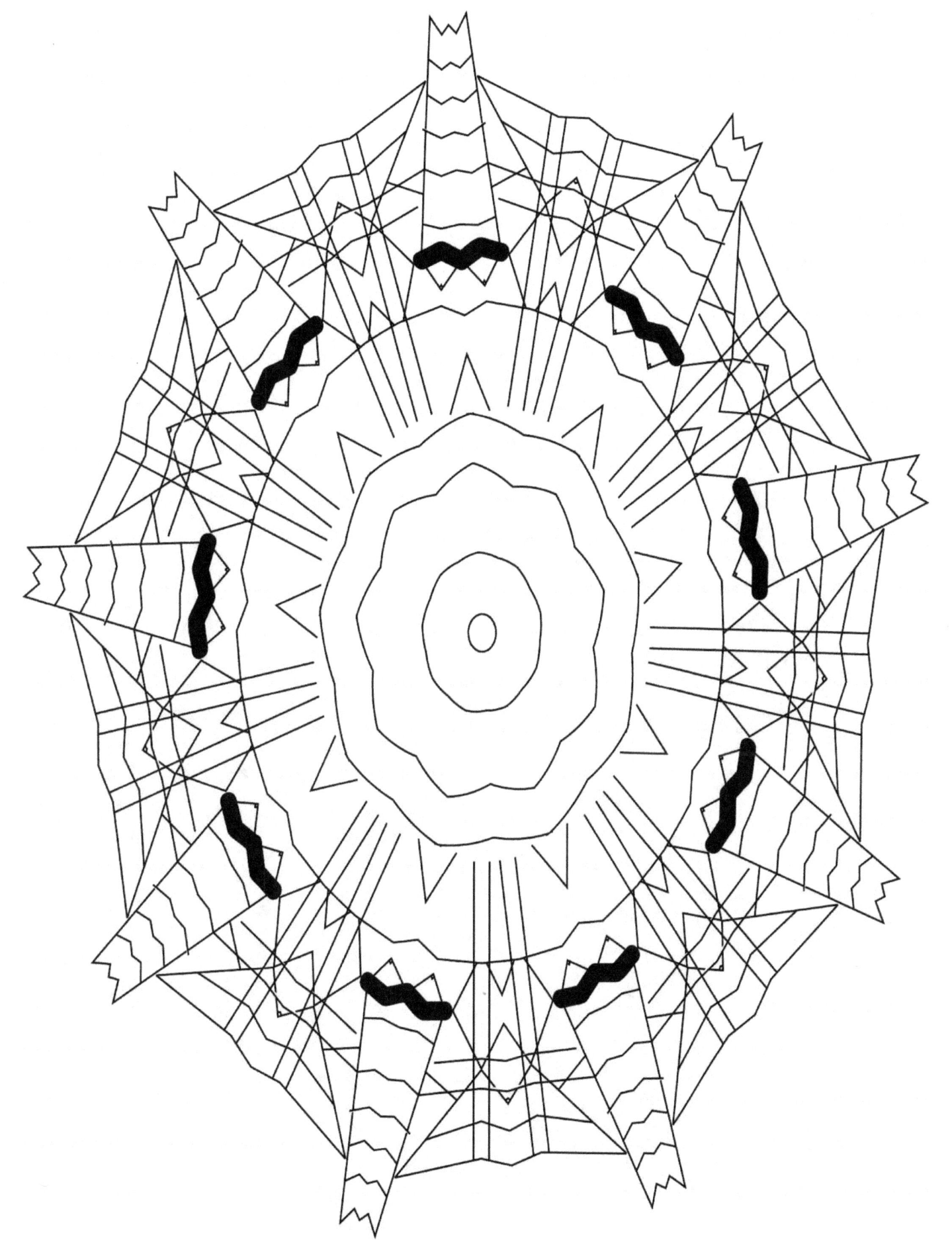

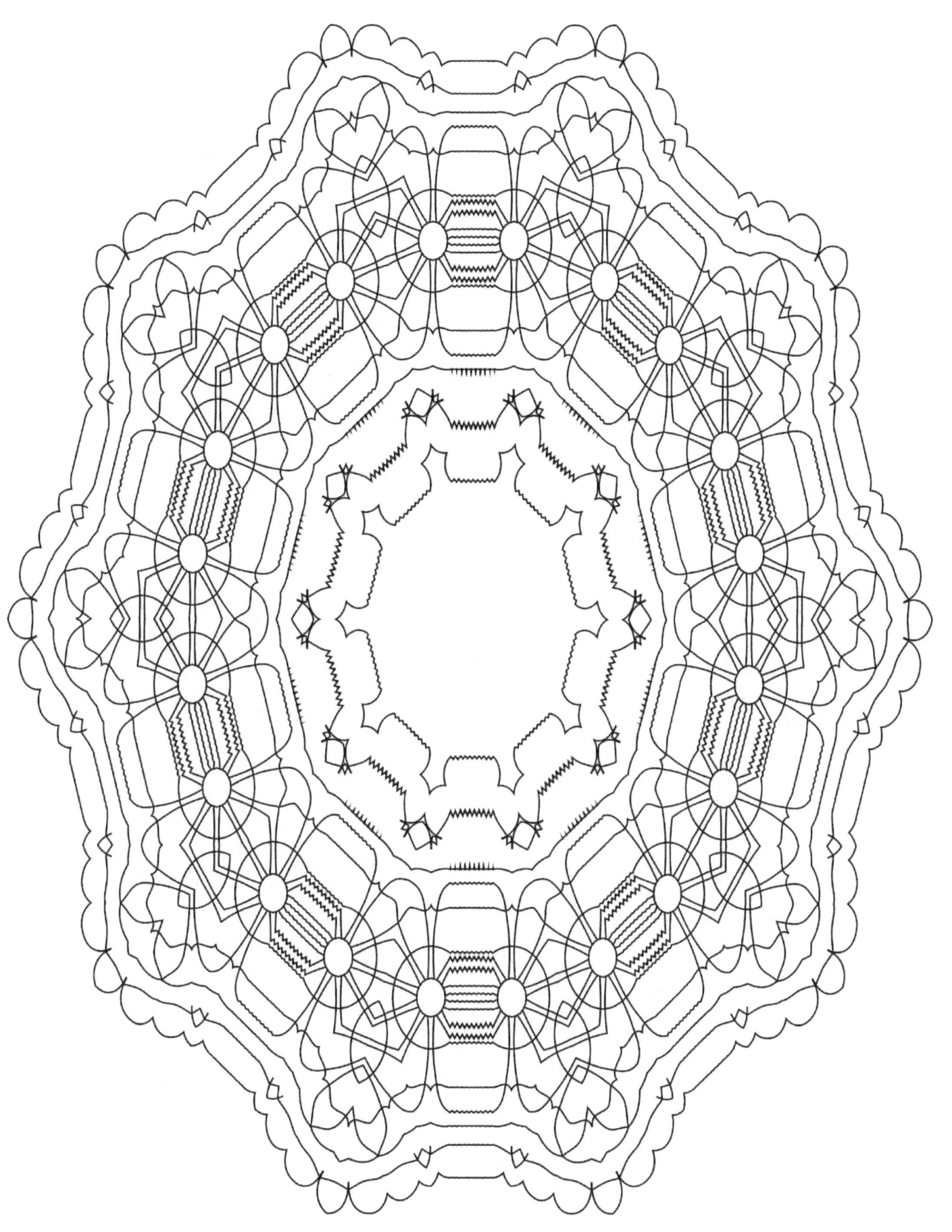

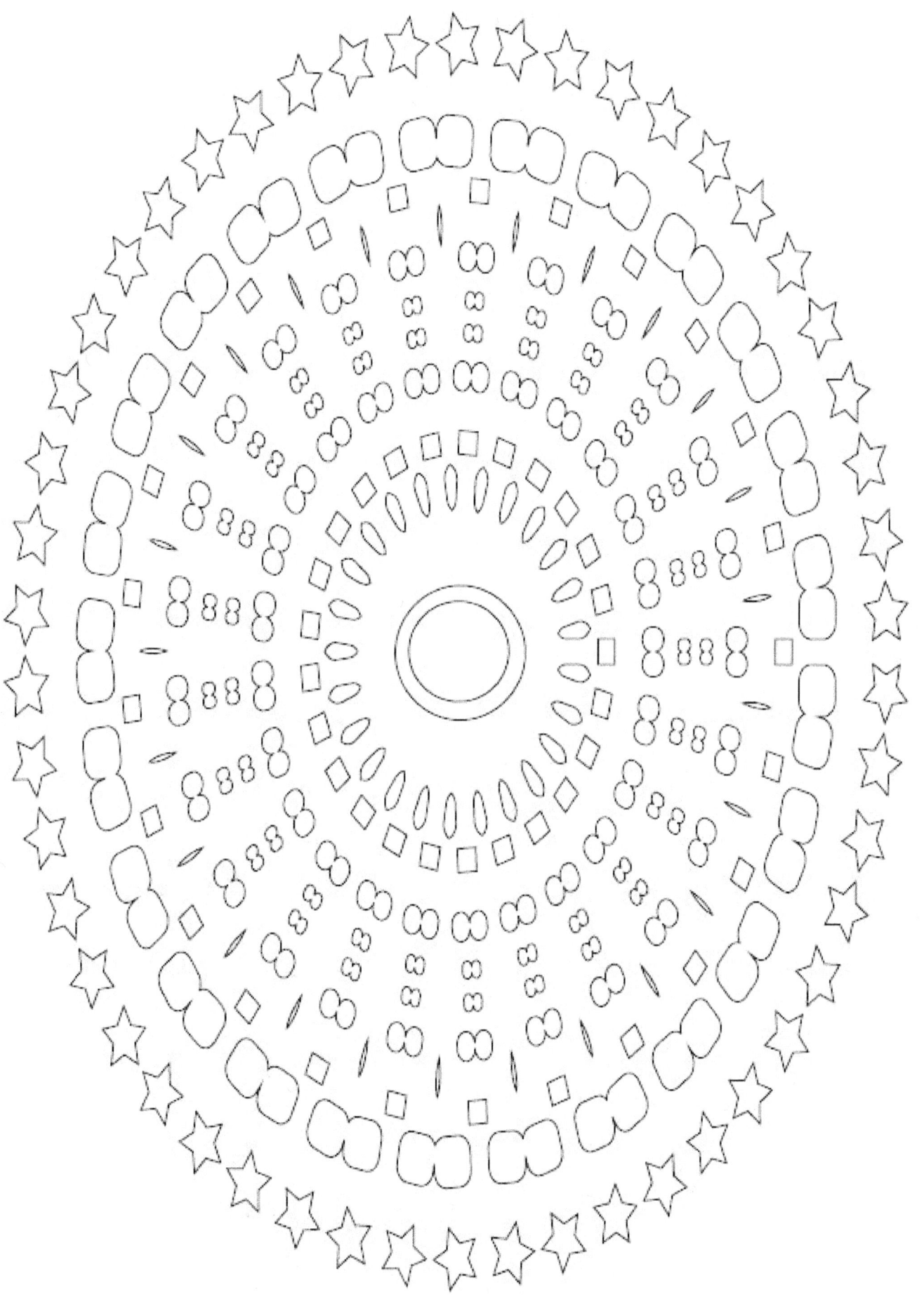

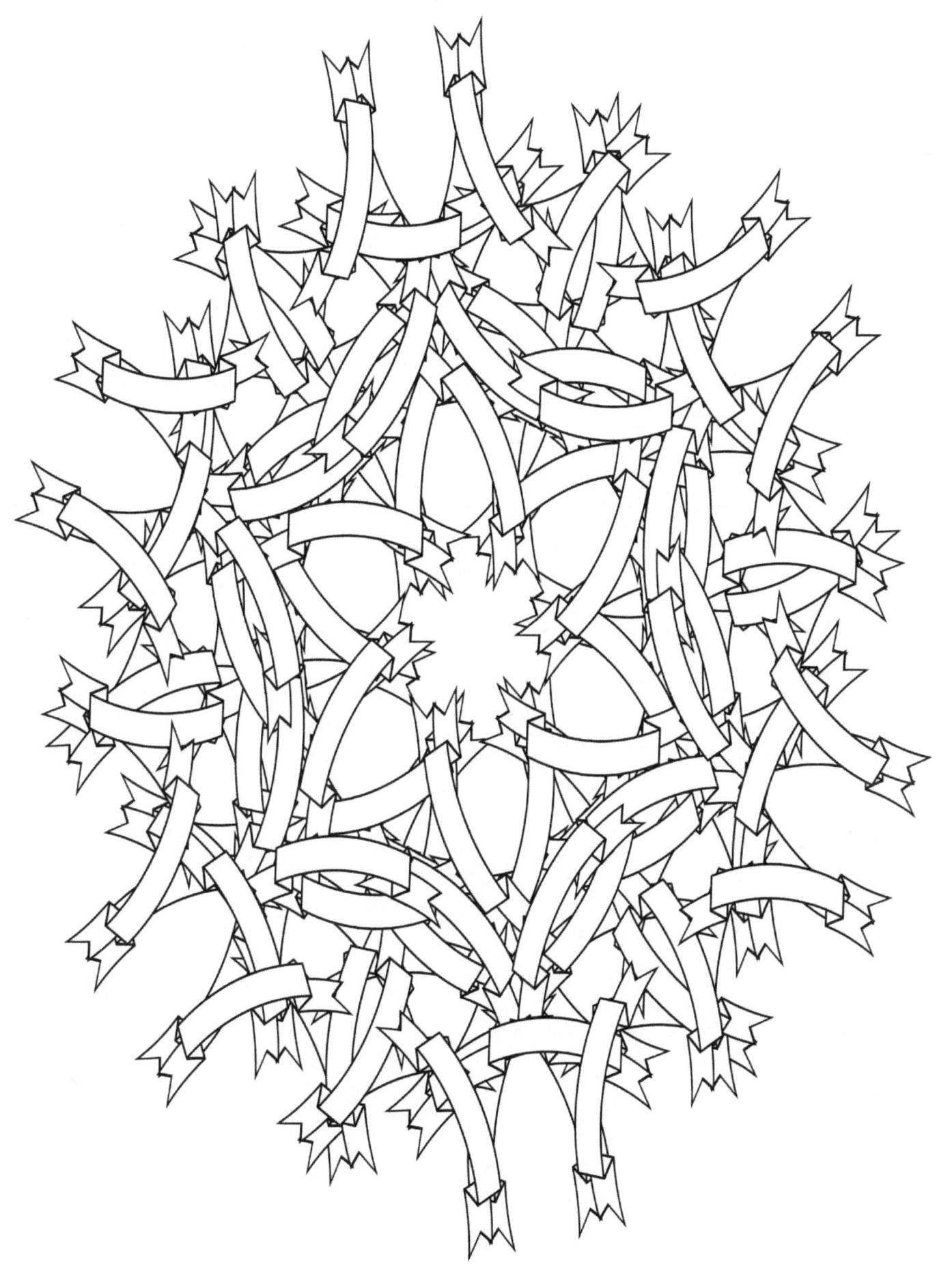

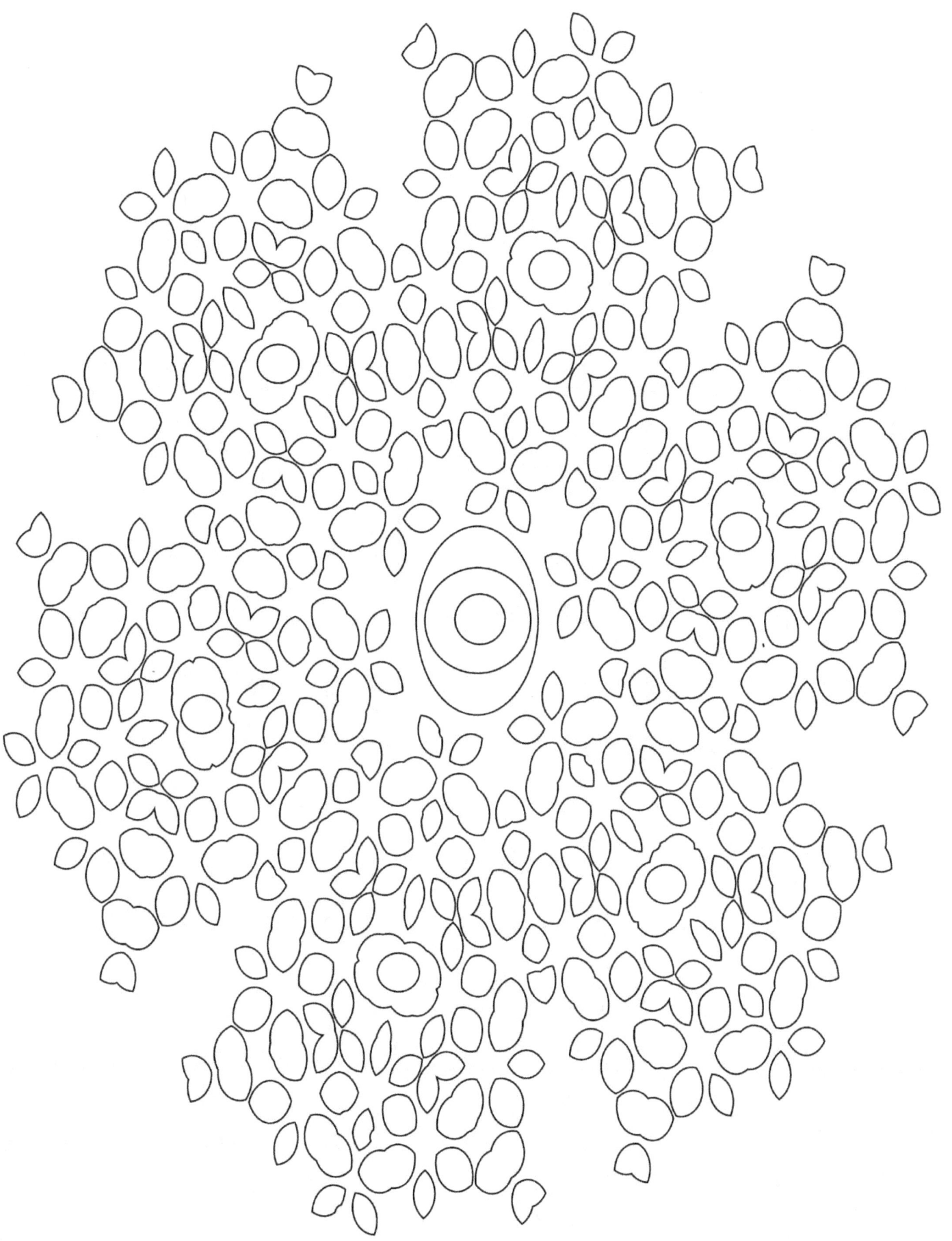

www.ingramcontent.com/pod-product-compliance
Lightning Source LLC
Chambersburg PA
CBHW081135290526
45795CB00006B/2243